SYRIA

Long-term detention and torture of political prisoners

AI Index MDE 24/12/92

ISBN: 0 86210 217 0

First published: July 1992

Amnesty International
 Publications
1 Easton Street
London WC1X 8DJ
United Kingdom

Printed by:
 Flashprint Enterprises Ltd.

Copyright:
 Amnesty International
 Publications

Original language: English

All rights reserved

No part of this publication may be reproduced, stored in a retrieval system, or transmitted in any form or by any means electronic, mechanical, photo-copying, recording and/or otherwise, without the prior permission of the publishers

CONTENTS

	Introduction	01
1	**Recent imprisonments and detentions**	05
	Imprisoned after unfair trial	05
	Recent detentions of political suspects	09
2	**Long-term untried political detainees**	11
	Former government and Ba'th Party officials	13
	Prohibited political organizations	15
	Professional associations	25
3	**Prisoners held beyond expiry of sentence**	27
4	**Torture and deaths in custody since 1987**	31
5	**Conclusions and Amnesty International's proposals**	34
	Amnesty International's proposals	39
	Endnotes	42
	Appendix: State of emergency laws	46

INTRODUCTION

When up to 2,000 political prisoners were suddenly and unexpectedly released from Syrian jails earlier this year, the dramatic scale of past human rights violations was made abundantly clear. Some of those freed had been held for more than two decades. Others had been held for years without even knowing why they had been arrested. Many said they had been tortured while held in prolonged incommunicado detention.

But the mass releases also offered hope — that a new era was beginning in Syria in which past wrongs would be righted and human rights would at last be respected.

This report shows that such hope may be premature, or even misplaced. Even as the announced releases were taking place in late 1991 and early 1992, hundreds of other political suspects and human rights activists were being arrested: several of them remain in prison, some without charge or trial. In addition, thousands of long-term political prisoners are still locked up in Syrian jails, including many prisoners of conscience detained solely for peacefully expressing their opposition to the government of President Hafez al-Assad. Moreover, nothing has been done to change the legislation and practices which allowed for such gross violations of human rights in the past.

The mass releases followed two presidential amnesties announced in December 1991 and March 1992. A total of 3,464 political prisoners were pardoned in the amnesties, but Amnesty International has only been able to confirm the actual release of around 2,000 between December 1991 and April 1992. No information has been received that the remainder have been freed, and requests by Amnesty International for full details of all releases have not been answered.

SYRIA

The freed prisoners had been held under state of emergency legislation which has been in force for nearly 30 years[1]. The legislation allows for indefinite detention without charge or trial of anyone suspected of "endangering security and public order".

Some of these freed prisoners who have now settled abroad described to Amnesty International what they had suffered under this legislation. Many were held for months or years without any contact with the outside world, including their families or lawyers. Many say they were tortured by a wide variety of methods, including beatings and electric shocks. Some reported that while in detention they repeatedly asked to be informed of the charges against them and brought to trial, or released. None was ever given a response.

Amnesty International is extremely concerned that the fundamental causes of such grave human rights violations remain unchanged. It is also concerned about the continued use of the death penalty and executions, and "disappearances".

In light of the wide publicity concerning the recent mass releases of political prisoners, this report focuses on the continuing use of the state of emergency powers to arbitrarily arrest and detain suspected political opponents of the government, and to deny them their most fundamental rights. It does not deal directly with other human rights violations in Syria. Nor does it deal directly with the violations of human rights in Lebanon by Syrian forces, which have included arbitrary arrests and detention, torture and ill-treatment of detainees, "disappearances" and extrajudicial executions committed against Lebanese and other nationals. All these concerns have been documented elsewhere by Amnesty International during the past few years. However, Amnesty International reiterates its many appeals to the Syrian authorities to address these concerns and calls on them to implement its recommendations as a matter of urgency.

This report summarizes Amnesty International's most recent information about political prisoners in Syria, as of late May 1992. It shows that three months after the second presidential amnesty, an estimated several thousand prisoners of conscience and political prisoners remain held, most of them without charge or trial, including around 500 whose names and details are known to the organization. Some were arrested shortly after the December 1991 amnesty. The majority, however, were arrested in the past two decades, in one case as far back as 1969.

INTRODUCTION

The prisoners include human rights activists, former government officials, members of professional associations and suspected political opponents of the present government. Most were arrested in connection with prohibited political organizations such as *Hizb al-'Amal al-Shuyu'i* (Party for Communist Action), *al-Hizb al-Shuyu'i al-Maktab al-Siyassi* (the Communist Party Political Bureau), *Hizb al-Ba'ath al-Dimoqrati al-Ishtiraki al-'Arabi* (the Arab Socialist Democratic Ba'th Party), *Hizb al-Ittihad al-'Arabi al-Ishtiraki fi-Suriya* (Arab Socialist Union Party in Syria), *al-Ikhwan al-Muslimun* (the Muslim Brotherhood), and pan-Arab (Nasserist) groups.

All the cases of prisoners of conscience and political prisoners known to Amnesty International follow a similar pattern. They were detained by *al-Mukhabarat al-'Askariyya*, Military Intelligence, or *al-Amn al-Siyassi*, Political Security, or other security forces which enjoy wide powers under the state of emergency. They were invariably arrested without a warrant and without their families being informed of the reasons for their arrest. They have then been held in circumstances which violate the most basic prisoners' rights guaranteed by international standards and some aspects of Syria's own laws.

Most have been detained without charge or trial, some for over 20 years, and have never been brought before a judge or offered the opportunity to challenge the lawfulness of their detention before a court of law. Some have been sentenced to terms of imprisonment by courts whose procedures fail to satisfy international standards for fair trial, such as those guaranteeing the right of defence and appeal. Others are still held after the expiry of their sentences.

In all cases known to Amnesty International, prisoners were subjected to prolonged incommunicado detention after arrest, some for the entire duration of their detention or imprisonment. Most were allegedly tortured; some are reported to be suffering from long-term illnesses as a result. Many such prisoners, and others who fall ill in prison, are denied adequate medical treatment. Over the years, dozens of prisoners have died in custody as a result of harsh prison conditions and torture.

Amnesty International has over the years repeatedly raised these issues with the Syrian authorities. In written appeals as well as in meetings with government officials and Syrian diplomats abroad, Amnesty International has persistently urged the release of all prisoners of conscience and the prompt, fair trial or release of all

SYRIA

other political prisoners. It has called on the Syrian authorities to initiate impartial investigations into all allegations of torture and deaths in custody, and sought guarantees that prisoners are receiving adequate medical care. However, no substantive response to any of these communications has been received from the authorities.

In 1980, for example, Amnesty International requested information about political detainees whose cases it believed should be reviewed by the authorities. It received no response. In 1989 an Amnesty International delegation met the Syrian Vice President in Damascus. It submitted lists of political detainees, requesting information about them. Although a response was promised, none was received. More recently, Amnesty International wrote to the authorities welcoming the presidential amnesties and asking for the names of all those released to be made public. Again, no response was received.

Amnesty International is publishing this report to draw international attention to continuing grave abuses of the rights of prisoners of conscience and other political prisoners in Syria. In doing so, it again calls on the Syrian authorities to take urgent steps to ensure that this pattern of human rights violations, which has persisted for nearly 30 years, is finally brought to an end.

1

Recent imprisonments and detentions

The mass releases of political prisoners in early 1992 raised hopes that the Syrian authorities were finally taking steps to end the long-term pattern of arbitrary arrest and detention of political opponents. But these hopes were almost immediately thrown into doubt by new arrests of suspected opponents of the government.

Between the two amnesties of December 1991 and March 1992, hundreds of political suspects and human rights activists were arrested by members of *al-Mukhabarat al-'Askariyya*, Military Intelligence, and *al-Amn al-Siyassi*, Political Security. Many were held for a short period and then released after interrogation, but at least 24 continue to be held.

Of the 24, 10 are now serving prison terms after an unfair trial: most of them are human rights activists. The other 14 are reported to be detained without charge or trial in connection with prohibited political organizations or suspected individual political activities. All 28 have been held incommunicado and the whereabouts of some of them are unknown. Some are alleged to have been severely tortured.

These cases indicate that, despite the welcome releases, nothing has been done to end the pattern of grave violations of the rights of political detainees and prisoners which have persisted in Syria for nearly 30 years.

Imprisoned after unfair trial

The 10 people serving sentences after an unfair trial were among 17 people arrested in December 1991 and January 1992 in connection with the Committees for the Defence of Democratic Freedoms and Human Rights in Syria (CDF). The CDF, a voluntary organization set up in 1989, has been campaigning for the abolition of the state of emergency in

Syria, the release of all political prisoners, and for greater respect for individual freedoms.

The 17 were held incommunicado in pre-trial detention in *Fara' al-Tahqiq al-'Askari*, Military Interrogation Branch, in Damascus. Some of them were severely tortured. Aktham Nu'aysa, a 41-year-old lawyer, was reportedly tortured so badly that he needed medical treatment and was admitted in early January to Harasta Military Hospital near Damascus.

All 17 were tried by the Supreme State Security Court[2] between 29 February and 17 March. This court is not bound by any existing judicial procedural rules applicable in ordinary criminal cases: only the right of defence is guaranteed, in principle, to the defendant.

In light of this, Amnesty International sought assurances from the Syrian authorities that the 17 defendants would receive a fair trial, as guaranteed by international human rights standards. Specifically, the organization requested that the defendants be given immediate access to lawyers of their own choice and sufficient opportunity to prepare their cases; that the trial should be held in public; and that if convicted the defendants be allowed to appeal to a higher tribunal. The organization also sought authorization to send observers to the trial, but this was denied.

Three of the defendants were acquitted and released. Fourteen were sentenced to prison terms ranging between three and 10 years. They were convicted on three separate charges: dissemination of false information, receiving money from abroad, and the withholding of information.

The accusation of dissemination of false information related to a leaflet issued and distributed by the CDF on 10 December 1991. The leaflet protested against human rights violations in Syria and criticized the procedure used for the re-election of President Hafez al-Assad at the beginning of December 1991.

The charge of disseminating false information was formulated on the basis of Article 3(e) of Legislative Decree No.6 of 7 January 1965, amended by Legislative Decree No.47 of 28 March 1968. The crime is punishable by imprisonment with hard labour for between three and 15 years, according to Article 44 of the Syrian Penal Code. Under Article 3(e) the leaflet and CDF activities were considered to be a crime of "...publication of false information intended to create anxiety and to shake the confidence of the masses in the aims of the revolution." (The revolution referred to is that of 8 March

CHAPTER 1

Aktham Nu'aysa (left), a lawyer and human rights activist, is serving a nine-year prison sentence imposed after an unfair trial. He was one of 14 defendants, most of them human rights activists, who were sentenced to between three and 10 years' imprisonment in March 1992. 'Abd al-'Aziz al-Khayyir (below left), a doctor, has been detained without charge or trial since February 1992 in connection with his alleged membership of the Party for Communist Action. Jamal Salih Sa'id (below right), a former university student, has been held since February or March 1992. His arrest was said to be connected to alleged political activities.

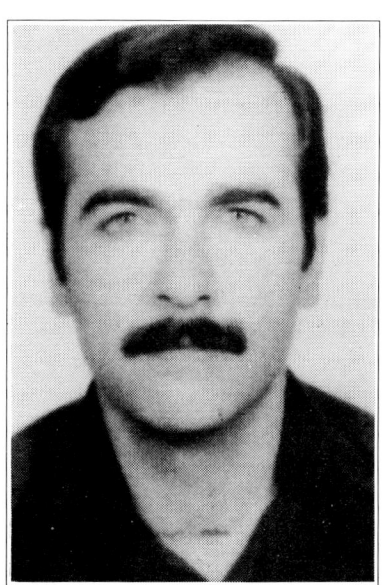

1963, when the Ba'th party assumed power in Syria.)

The charge of receiving money from abroad reportedly related to about 25,000 Syrian Lira (about £700) sent to one of the main defendants, Aktham Nu'aysa, by a brother of his who lives in Europe. The prosecution charged that the money was to finance the activities of the CDF and as such was a crime under Article 3(f) of Legislative Decree No.6 of 7 January 1965. This crime is punishable by death under Article 4(d) of the same decree.

The charge relating to the withholding of information was brought against some defendants on the grounds that they were aware of the distribution of the CDF leaflet and possibly the money transfer and failed to inform the authorities. Such non-disclosure is considered a crime against the security of the state under Article 388 of the Syrian Penal Code, punishable by imprisonment for between one and three years and deprivation of civil rights.

Ten of the 14 were convicted of disseminating false information and receiving money from abroad. They were sentenced to prison terms ranging from five to 10 years with deprivation of their civil rights. Among them are Nizar Nayyuf, a 36-year-old sociologist and writer, and Aktham Nu'aysa, who were sentenced respectively to 10 and nine years' imprisonment. The other four were convicted of withholding information and were sentenced to three years' imprisonment each: they were released in late May 1992 under the presidential amnesty announced two months earlier.

The trial was held *in camera*, although some relatives of the defendants were allowed to attend the last session of the court hearings which was devoted mainly to the pronouncement of the verdict. The defendants were assisted by about 11 lawyers, all chosen by their families. However, the lawyers were apparently not allowed prior consultation with the defendants and were said to have been allowed to meet them only in court during the hearings.

The evidence produced by the prosecution consisted of confessions, said to have been extracted under torture, and copies of the CDF leaflet of 10 December 1991. Two of the defendants, Aktham Nu'aysa and Nizar Nayyuf, were apparently not able to walk into the court room unaided as a result of the severe torture to which they had allegedly been subjected. The prosecution demanded the death sentence for the 10 defendants whose charges included receiving money from abroad. Defence lawyers requested postponement of the trial and adequate time to prepare their case and produce witnesses, but this was not granted.

The defendants were not allowed to appeal against their conviction and sentences as the Supreme State Security Court's decisions are final. Legally, the sentences cannot be enforced before they have been ratified by President Hafez al-Assad, who may suspend the verdict, order a retrial or reduce the penalty[3]. At the time of writing, Amnesty International was not aware whether the ratification had taken place, although all 10 prisoners continued to be held incommunicado, reportedly in Saidnaya prison.

Amnesty International has called for the immediate and unconditional release of all 10 prisoners. It believes they are prisoners of conscience, held solely for the non-violent expression of their conscientiously held beliefs. The organization had not received a response by the end of May.

Recent detentions of political suspects

The 14 other people arrested in connection with prohibited political organizations or suspected political activities are reported to be held without charge or trial in incommunicado detention. Their exact whereabouts are unknown, although some of them are believed to be in *Fara' al-Tahqiq al-'Askari*, Military Interrogation Branch, and *Fara' Falastin*, Palestine Branch — both detention centres in Damascus. Nine are reported to be held for membership of prohibited political organizations; five are said to have been suspected of individual political activities.

Seven of the nine held in connection with prohibited political organizations are apparently detained for membership of *Hizb al-'Amal al-Shuyu'i*, the Party for Communist Action (PCA). They were arrested at the beginning of February and in March in various towns and cities. They include 'Abd al-'Aziz al-Khayyir, a 41-year-old doctor, married with one child, and Bahjat Sha'bu, a 34-year-old former medical student, also married with one child. They are said to have been arrested on 1 February in Suq al-Hamidiyya Street in Damascus. The authorities had reportedly been seeking their arrest for some time in connection with activities related to the PCA. Bahjat Sha'bu had previously been detained between 1979 and 1980, also in connection with PCA activities. The wives of both detainees, Muna al-Ahmad and Rana Ilyas Mahfudh respectively, are former prisoners of conscience. They had been detained without charge or trial for many years and were released in December 1991 along with some 60 other women prisoners of conscience.

SYRIA

The other two of the nine are reported to be detained in connection with *al-Tanzim al-Sha'bi al-Dimoqrati al-Nasiri*, the Nasserist Democratic Popular Organization (NDPO). They are Ahmad Ma'tuq, an employee of Damascus City Council married with four children, and Marwan Ghazi, the owner of a publishing house. They were reportedly arrested in March and their exact whereabouts are unknown.

The five believed to be held for their individual political activity were also arrested in February and March. Four of them had previously been detained for long periods without charge or trial, reportedly for membership of or sympathy with the PCA. They include two 33-year-old former university students and former prisoners of conscience, Jaffan Humsi and Jamal Salih Sa'id. Both men had been in continuous detention from 1980 and 1981 respectively until April 1991, when they were released along with dozens of others held in connection with the PCA. The four are said to have had no links with the PCA since their release from previous detention. Their current whereabouts have not been confirmed but they are believed to be held at *Fara' al-Tahqiq al-'Askari* or *Fara' Falastin*.

The fifth detainee, Salama George Kila, a 37-year-old Palestinian writer and journalist, was reportedly summoned to the headquarters of *al-Amn al-Siyassi* in the al-Maysat area of Damascus on 12 March. He has been held since then. According to Amnesty International's information, he has never belonged to any political organization, but he is thought to have been suspected by the authorities of having been involved in preparing press articles about Syria, which were published in Jordan shortly before his arrest. His whereabouts are unknown, but he may still be held in the headquarters of *al-Amn al-Siyassi* in the al-Maysat area of Damascus.

Amnesty International is concerned that all 14 detainees may be subject to torture, not least because they are being denied all contact with the outside world. It is also concerned that they may be in detention solely for the non-violent expression of their conscientiously held beliefs, and has called for them to be released if this is the case. The organization has issued urgent appeals seeking assurances that they are being treated humanely, given regular access to their families and lawyers while in detention, and provided with proper medical treatment if necessary. No substantive response has been received from the Syrian authorities.

2

Long-term untried political detainees

Thousands of prisoners of conscience and political prisoners are still locked away in Syrian jails. Most have been held without charge or trial for many years — some for more than two decades. They are detained under Article 4(a) of the State of Emergency Law, Legislative Decree 51 of 22 December 1962 (see Appendix I), which allows:

"The placing of restrictions on freedom of individuals with respect to meetings, residence, travel and passage in specific places or at particular times. Preventive arrest of anyone suspected of endangering public security and order. Authorization to investigate persons and places. Delegation of any person to perform any of these tasks."

All were arrested without warrant by members of the security forces. A typical example was described to Amnesty International by a relative of a political detainee who remains in prison since his arrest in 1980:

"Secret agents from the government came to my paternal grandmother's house and hid outside waiting for him to come out. When they arrested him there was no warrant and no reason given for the arrest."

In a separate case, relatives of another detainee arrested in 1980 told Amnesty International in 1990:

"Secret agents from the government came to the hospital where he was working and took him away. There was no arrest warrant and no reason given for the arrest."

Almost all such detainees have then been held incommunicado and some continue to be denied all access to the outside world. Relatives of one detainee, held since 1980, told Amnesty International in 1990:

"The last time we heard anything about him

SYRIA

> was about five years ago when some prisoners that had been released came to our home to tell my parents that he was still alive.... He simply disappeared one day and has only been heard from twice. We have had no information about him regarding charges, defence or trial."

A Palestinian former detainee who had been held in *Fara' Falastin* from July 1987 to March 1991 told Amnesty International that the first time he had access to his family was three months after his arrest. He said this was quick by the standard practice of that detention centre. Another former detainee, also a Palestinian, who had been held there in the same period, told the organization that he saw his family for the first time a year after his arrest. He said that his family did not know where he was until a few months after his arrest. His mother learned from relatives of other detainees where he was. She went to *Fara' Falastin* several times but was told he was not held there.

It is not uncommon for relatives to wait months or years to discover the whereabouts of detainees. Some are still waiting.

One father of a detainee who has been in detention since 1982 told Amnesty International in 1990:

> "Eight years ago I met by chance someone who said they had seen my son, ill, in Palmyra Prison. But multiple attempts to get information from the authorities have been futile — I have been unable to contact or get information about my son."

Almost all detainees are held without any recourse to justice. Some are understood to have made repeated requests to be tried or released, but have not had any response to their demands. They continue to be held without being given any reason or legal basis for their detention.

Many of the detainees have allegedly been tortured, causing injuries or long-term health problems. In addition, many fall ill in prison, particularly those held for prolonged periods in extremely trying circumstances. Such prisoners are often denied adequate medical treatment, exacerbating illnesses and sometimes resulting in premature death. Amnesty International has frequently received information from former detainees and relatives of current detainees about such lack of medical treatment, and has sent numerous urgent appeals to the government asking for treatment to be made available.

CHAPTER 2

Among the thousands of political detainees still held are former government and Ba'th Party officials, members and suspected members or sympathizers of various opposition organizations, and members of professional associations.

Examples of such detainees are given in the following sections.

Former government and Ba'th Party officials

Seventeen former government and Ba'th Party officials have been held without charge or trial since their arrest over 20 years ago. Sixteen of them were arrested shortly after the coup which brought President Assad to power in November 1970 — all were leading figures in the government which was overthrown. The other detainee, former army officer Ahmad Suwaidani, was arrested in 1969 by the previous government but continues to be held.

Ahmad Suwaidani, a diplomat and member of the Ba'th Party Regional Command, was arrested on 11 July at Damascus Airport after returning from Iraq. He was suspected of being a pro-Iraqi Ba'thist. Since then he has been detained in al-Mezze Military Prison in Damascus where he has been allowed family visits. He is now 63 years old. In July 1989, to mark his 20 years in detention, he went on hunger-strike to demand his release. However, he is still held without charge or trial. He is reported to be in poor health.

The 16 former government and Ba'th party officials were among a larger group of members and supporters of the former government who were arrested in 1970 and 1971. They had reportedly refused to cooperate with the new authorities after the coup. Many have been released since then, some of them in recent amnesties. For example, Yousuf al-Burji, a 53-year-old Palestinian of Jordanian nationality, was released in early April after the March 1992 presidential amnesty. Salman 'Abdallah, a former member of the National Command of the Ba'th Party in Syria, was released in September 1991. Both had been held continuously without charge or trial since 1971.

The 16 who remain in detention include Syria's former head of state, Dr Nour al-Din al-Atassi, who was also Secretary General of the Ba'th Party. He was arrested, at the age of 41, in November 1970 immediately after the coup. He is now 63. At the end of April 1992 he was reported to have suffered a heart attack and was admitted

SYRIA

Clockwise from above left: Ahmad Suwaidani, seen here aged about 40, has been held without charge or trial since his arrest at Damascus airport in July 1969. He is now 63. A former army officer and diplomat, he was also a member of the Ba'ath Party Regional Command. Nour al-Din al-Atassi (above right) is the former head of state of Syria. He has been held since his arrest in November 1970 following the coup which brought the present government to power. Hakem al-Faiz, a Jordanian national and member of the National Command of the Ba'ath Party, was abducted from Lebanon in 1971 and has since been held in al-Mezze Military Prison. Salah Jadid, the former assistant secretary general of the Regional Command of the Ba'th Party, was also arrested shortly after the 1970 coup and remains in prison.

to Tishrin Military Hospital in Damascus. While being treated he was apparently found to have intestinal polyps for which he needs surgery.

Hakem al-Faiz, a Jordanian national and until the coup a member of the National Command of the Syrian Ba'th Party, went to live in Lebanon after the coup. In 1971 he was abducted by Syrian security agents, taken to Syria and detained. He was reportedly held incommunicado for seven months before being allowed family visits. In August 1991 he was moved from prison and restricted to a house in Damascus, where his family was able to stay with him. This raised expectations that his release was imminent, but in October 1991 he was returned to al-Mezze Military Prison. He is said to be suffering from acute depression.

The other 14 are also said to be in poor health due to inadequate medical facilities and prolonged imprisonment. Muhammad 'Id 'Ashawi reportedly suffers from acute anaemia, rheumatism and a stomach ulcer. A former minister of foreign affairs, now aged 62, he has been detained without charge or trial since December 1970.

All 16 prisoners are detained in al-Mezze Military Prison in Damascus where they are allowed family visits once a month. Amnesty International considers all to be prisoners of conscience and has repeatedly called for their immediate and unconditional release.

Prohibited political organizations

Most prisoners of conscience and political prisoners in Syria are held on account of their suspected links to various prohibited political organizations. They include suspected members and sympathizers of the Muslim Brotherhood, non-official wings of the Ba'th Party, the PCA, Communist Party Political Bureau (CPPB), and two Nasserist organizations.

The Muslim Brotherhood:

Several thousand people have been arrested in connection with the Muslim Brotherhood and many are still being detained, although Amnesty International cannot determine the exact number.

Some have been held since the 1970s, but the majority were arrested in the early 1980s following violent clashes between the security forces and armed wings of the Muslim Brotherhood. Many have been tortured and some have reportedly died in custody as a result.

SYRIA

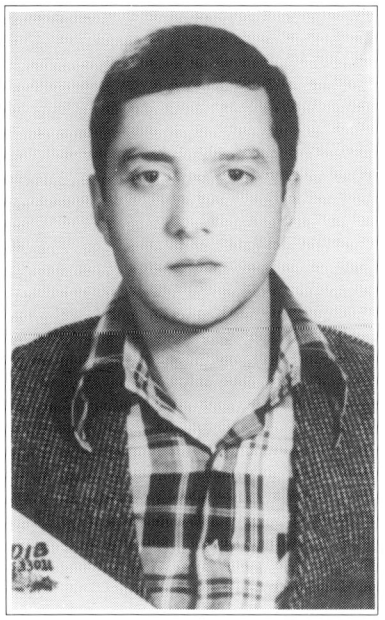

Al-Hakam Karkoukli (left), now aged 36, was arrested in 1977 for suspected membership of the Muslim Brotherhood. He is believed to be in Saidnaya Prison. Muhammad Reem al-Basha (below left), now aged 35, was detained in 1979 also on suspicion of belonging to the Muslim Brotherhood: he is still believed held but his whereabouts are unknown. Bara al-Sarrat (below right), now aged 28, was arrested in March 1984 and has since been detained, apparently for being the nephew of a leading member of the Muslim Brotherhood.

CHAPTER 2

In July 1980 the government passed Law 49 making membership of the Muslim Brotherhood a crime punishable by death. The law was passed in the wake of violent clashes between the security forces and armed members of the Muslim Brotherhood which began in the late 1970s and intensified in early 1980. Several hundred civilians died in the clashes and government officials were assassinated by armed members of the Muslim Brotherhood. Scores of members of the armed forces were also killed. The security forces carried out mass arrests and committed indiscriminate killings in various parts of the country, particularly in the towns of Jisr al-Shughur and Sarmada. Between 600 and 1,200 suspected Muslim Brotherhood supporters who had been arrested were reportedly shot dead in June 1980 in Tadmur Military Prison, where they were being held.

The crackdown by the security forces continued into 1982, culminating in the Hama massacre in February that year. At the beginning of February some 90 soldiers were ambushed in Hama and killed by armed *Mujahideen*, one of the armed groups of the Muslim Brotherhood. This was followed by the occupation and ransacking of government and security forces' buildings. Some government officials and "collaborators" were summarily killed, reportedly by members of the Muslim Brotherhood. The authorities responded by deploying between 6,000 and 8,000 soldiers and security forces in the city, who then carried out mass killings. The clashes left an estimated 10,000 or more people dead, including many civilians.

Many of those arrested in connection with these events and with the Muslim Brotherhood in general, and who continue to be held, were not apparently involved in violent activities. They are said to have been arrested on suspicion of being members or sympathizers of the Muslim Brotherhood or because they were relatives of active members of the organization.

Among those still held on suspicion of being members of the Muslim Brotherhood are al-Hakam Karkoukli and Muhammad Zahed Derkal. Others, such as Muhammad Rim al-Basha and Ahmad Kalaji, have not been heard of since their arrest but are believed to be still held.

Al-Hakam Karkoukli, a former student now aged 36, was reportedly arrested on 25 November 1977 in al-Amawiyyin Square in Damascus by members of *al-Mukhabarat al-'Askariyya*. He was held incommunicado in al-Mezze Military Prison until 1979 when his family was allowed to visit him five times during the year. From 1979 to 1989 he was reportedly held in Tadmur Military Prison; his family had no contact with him and were not sure of his whereabouts. In 1990 his family learned from relatives of other prisoners that he was being held in Saidnaya Prison. Political detainees released from Saidnaya Prison following the December 1991 presidential amnesty have apparently confirmed that he is still held there.

Muhammad Zahed Derkal, a 33-year-old furniture-maker, was arrested in May or June 1980 reportedly by 15 plainclothes security men at the Abu-Khair Mosque in Damascus. They were said to have shot him twice in the foot while making the arrest. He is believed to have since been held incommunicado. His exact whereabouts remained unknown until 1986, when former detainees said he was being held in Tadmur Military Prison. Amnesty International does not know whether he is still there.

Muhammad Rim al-Basha, a former student now aged 35, is believed to have been arrested in July 1979. His family have not seen or heard of him since and his whereabouts are unknown.

Ahmad Kalaji, a 38-year-old engineer married with two children, has not been heard of since his arrest in November 1980 in al-Qataifa village near Damascus. Family inquiries about his whereabouts remain unanswered by the authorities. Ahmad Kalaji is said to have been detained for a month in early 1980 prior to his second arrest.

Among those thought to be held because of their family connection with members of the Muslim Brotherhood is Bara al-Sarraj, a 28-year-old former student of engineering at the University of Damascus. On 5 March 1984 he went to the university as usual, but did not return. Following inquiries, his family learned that he had been taken away by members of *al-Mukhabarat al-'Askariyya* from the main lecture hall. He was detained briefly in Damascus before being transferred to a prison in Hama where his family was allowed to visit him for about two months. Subsequently, he was transferred to Tadmur Military Prison where he has since been held without any family visits. As far as Amnesty International is aware, no official reason has been given for his arrest and detention. However, he is the nephew of 'Adnan Sa'd al-Din, a leading member of the Muslim Brotherhood who lives in exile, and his relatives believe this is the reason for his detention. Bara al-Sarraj suffers from a respiratory illness and is said to have little opportunity to exercise.

In October 1991 Amnesty International sought assurances that he was receiving proper medical attention but did not receive a response from the Syrian Government.

The Arab Socialist Democratic Ba'th Party:
Up to 40 political detainees continue to be held in connection with *Hizb al-Ba'th al-Dimoqrati al-Ishtiraki al-'Arabi*, the Arab Socialist Democratic Ba'th Party. This party is a breakaway faction from the official *Hizb al-Ba'th al-'Arabi al-Ishtiraki*, Socialist Arab Ba'th Party, which held power in Syria from February 1966 until the November 1970 coup. Most of the 16 detained former government and Ba'th Party officials referred to in Chapter 1 were the leaders of this faction. Since 1970, dozens of members and followers of this faction have been imprisoned for their political activities.

The 40 or so detainees currently known to be held were arrested at various times during the 1970s and early 1980s. They include writers, journalists, teachers and students. One of them, Ahmad Suwaidan, a journalist and writer in his fifties, has been in detention without charge or trial since 1980. He is reported to be held in al-Mezze Military Prison. He is also a trade unionist and the author of a book said to be critical of restrictions on trade union activities in Syria. It is not known whether he is allowed regular family visits.

The Party for Communist Action:
Up to 250 long-term untried political detainees, including prisoners of conscience, are believed to be currently held in connection with the PCA. All were arrested between 1980 and 1991 following waves of repression against the party's activities. PCA literature has frequently highlighted and condemned government violations of human rights and civil liberties. It has also called for the lifting of the state of emergency and for the introduction of democratic freedoms. In 1980, during the widespread violent clashes between the security forces and the armed wing of the Muslim Brotherhood, the PCA issued statements opposing the use of violence by both sides. Up to 1,000 members or suspected members and sympathizers of this party have been arrested, detained without trial and tortured in recent years.

The 250 or so who continue to be held in 1992, excluding the seven arrested recently (see Chapter 1), include people from various professions, particularly students, engineers, labourers, teachers, civil servants, soldiers, doctors and lawyers. Many of them have been detained for more than 10 years. Among them is

SYRIA

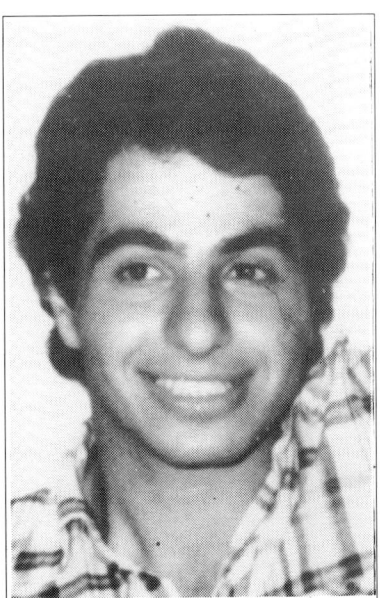

Munif Mulhim, Nahhas Nihad, Mustafa Khalifa and Ghassan Qassis (clockwise from above left) are all being held in connection with the Party for Communist Action.

CHAPTER 2

Munif Mulhim, a 41-year-old mechanical engineer, who has been detained without charge or trial since 1981. He is said to be suffering from severe genital inflammation, possibly caused by a genital tumour. He is held in Saidnaya Prison. In the same prison are three of his brothers, Munzir, Nabil and Yasser, who have all been held without charge or trial since their arrest in 1987.

Many of these detainees are alleged to have been tortured or ill-treated. Some are said to have sustained severe torture injuries and to be in poor health as a result. They include Nizar Maradni and Ghassan Qassis.

Nizar Maradni, a 35-year-old former tutor of engineering at the University of Damascus, was reportedly tortured in *Fara' Falastin* where he had been held following his arrest in September 1987. He is said to have been suspended from a ceiling by his wrists and later dropped to the floor, fracturing his pelvis. He was reportedly arrested because he and another engineer had sent a pamphlet to the Union of Engineers calling for the restoration of democratic freedoms in Syria.

Ghassan Qassis, a 31-year-old lecturer in civil engineering at the University of Damascus, was reportedly shot in the hands at the time of his arrest in September 1987. He was allegedly tortured shortly afterwards by being suspended from a ceiling by his wrists for prolonged periods, causing some paralysis.

Most of the 250 PCA detainees whose cases are known to Amnesty International are currently believed to be in Saidnaya, 'Adra and Aleppo prisons, where they are allowed family visits. However, the whereabouts of some of the 250 are not known to Amnesty International. It is unclear whether one of them, Mudar al-Jundi, a 34-year-old engineer from Tartus, is still alive. He was arrested on 20 September 1987 having been sought for arrest by the authorities since 1984. He was detained in *Fara' Falastin* and allegedly tortured, and has apparently not been seen by his family since his arrest. His wife, Munira al-Jundi, a civil engineer, is a former prisoner of conscience. She was arrested two months after her husband, in December 1987, and held until December 1991 when she was released along with some 60 other women prisoners of conscience. In September 1991, while still in prison, she apparently asked to see her husband. Security officers then reportedly went to Mudar al-Jundi's parents to ask his whereabouts. They told his parents that Mudar's wife had asked to see him. The parents were said to have protested at this since, as far as they were

SYRIA

Riad al-Turk (left), George Sabra (below left) and Muhammad Munir Missouti are among the many detainees held in connection with the Communist Party Political Bureau.

concerned, he was also in detention. The security officers apparently denied that Mudar al-Jundi was being detained by them. Relatives and friends of Mudar al-Jundi fear that he may have died in detention.

The Communist Party Political Bureau:
Over 30 political detainees, including prisoners of conscience, are currently held for membership or activities linked with the CPPB. Most of them were arrested in the early 1980s, particularly during the widespread violent clashes between the Muslim Brotherhood and the security forces. At that time the CPPB apparently publicly condemned the mass killings by the security forces, and called for the release of political prisoners and an end to torture. Like other opposition organizations, it has called for the lifting of the state of emergency and for greater democratic freedoms. More than 100 members or suspected members and sympathizers of the CPPB are known by Amnesty International to have been arrested, detained without trial and tortured in recent years.

Those who continue to be held in 1992 include the First Secretary of the party, Riad al-Turk, a 61-year-old lawyer. He was arrested on 28 October 1980 in al-Mezze in Damascus by members of *al-Amn al-Siyassi*. His wife, Dr Asmah al-Faisal, was detained a few days earlier. She remained in detention until the end of 1982 when she was released from Qatana Women's Prison in Damascus. However, Riad al-Turk continues to be held incommunicado in the Military Interrogation Branch in Damascus where he is said to have been repeatedly tortured, sustaining fractures to the arm and leg and a loss of hearing. He is also reported to have diabetes and other ailments which have periodically necessitated his being admitted for hospital treatment, including in March 1991. In 1988 it was reported that the Syrian authorities had set up a committee to look into his case in view of his deteriorating health. However, despite the gravity and the progressive nature of his condition, he continues to be held in the Military Interrogation Branch in Damascus.

According to information received by Amnesty International, at the beginning of 1992 his conditions of detention improved slightly. He has apparently been allowed books and newspapers. However, his health continues to cause grave anxiety. Medical facilities at the Military Interrogation Branch are said to be inadequate for the proper monitoring of Riad al-Turk's condition and for providing the medical care he needs.

Other CPPB detainees are held in various prisons and detention centres and most of them are believed to be allowed family visits. However, some of them are said to have been held incommunicado and tortured periodically to force them to denounce the CPPB's policies. They include 'Umar Qashash and Faisal Tahhan.

'Umar Qashash, a member of the politburo of the CPPB and former Secretary General of the Union of Printers, was arrested in October 1980 and is believed to be held in 'Adra Prison. In 1986 he was reportedly interrogated and tortured. He had previously been detained in 1978 and allegedly tortured severely, apparently resulting in serious lesions of the spinal column affecting his central nervous system.

Faisal Tahhan, a 48-year-old teacher, married with three children, was also arrested in 1980 and is currently believed to be in Saidnaya Prison. In 1986 Amnesty International received reports that he had been severely tortured while detained in Kafr Sousseh Prison in Damascus and that he had lost the sight of his left eye as a result.

Nasserist groups:

Most long-term political detainees held in connection with Nasserist political groups were released in December 1991. However, at least five are reported to be still held, excluding the two who have been detained since March 1992 (see Chapter 1).

Two of the five are said to be detained for membership of *Hizb al-Ittihad al-'Arabi al-Ishtiraki fi-Suriya*, the Arab Socialist Union Party in Syria (ASUPS). The ASUPS was founded in 1964 to work towards the unity of the Arab world as advocated and pursued by Jamal 'Abd al-Nasser, Egypt's President from 1952 to 1970. It has been critical of the Syrian Government and many of its members have over the years been imprisoned and tortured. Those who continue to be detained are 'Ali al-Rifa'i and 'Adil Sahyuni.

'Ali al-Rifa'i, a 42-year-old agricultural engineer from Dar'a, was reportedly arrested in February 1981. He is thought to be currently held in Dar'a Prison. 'Adil Sahyuni, a 48-year-old former employee of the Justice Palace in Aleppo, was reportedly arrested in July 1987. He is believed to be held in 'Adra Prison and is said to suffer from heart problems for which he does not receive regular medical attention.

Three other detainees are reported to be still held for membership of *al-Tanzim al-Sha'bi al-Dimoqrati al-Naseri*, the Nasserist Democratic Popular Organization (NDPO). The NDPO also advocates Arab unity as pursued by Jamal 'Abd al-Nasser. It was founded in 1978 in the wake of the visit to Jerusalem by Egypt's former President Anwar al-Sadat, and has been critical of the Syrian Government's internal and external policies. Many of its members have been detained and tortured. One, Rif'at bin Ahmad Rajab, died on 16 April 1992 of a heart condition for which he had allegedly received inadequate medical care.

The three NDPO members still held include Dr Khalid al-Nasser, a 47-year-old kidney specialist, who was arrested in September 1986 in Aleppo. He is believed to be at Muslimiyya Prison in Aleppo. He is said to be in poor health. In October 1991 Amnesty International sought assurances from the Syrian authorities that 'Adil Sahyuni and Dr Khalid al-Nasser were receiving proper medical attention, but did not receive a response. The other two — Muhammad Daqu, a 51-year-old lawyer, and 'Ali Ghabsha, a 53-year-old engineer — were reportedly arrested in 1986 and are now believed to be held at 'Adra and Aleppo prisons respectively.

Professional associations

Dozens of doctors and engineers are believed to remain in detention without charge or trial since their arrest more than 11 years ago. Their arrests occurred in the wake of a one-day general strike on 31 March 1980, which was organized by the Damascus branch of the Syrian Bar Association and supported by various professional associations. They called for political reforms, including an end to the state of emergency in Syria and the human rights violations committed under the state of emergency legislation.

The strike was the culmination of a movement for reform initiated by lawyers in Damascus in 1978. They were seeking to amend the emergency legislation to prevent human rights abuses, to reinstate the effective role of the judiciary and to protect the rights of the individual.

During the one-day national strike, shops, schools, universities and businesses were shut. In Damascus the security forces went out in large numbers and forced businesses to remain open. Similar attempts were made in other Syrian cities and led to clashes in the streets between security forces and demonstrators.

Shortly after the strike, a Presidential Decree was issued recommending the dissolution of the professional associations' councils. On 9 April 1980 the Ministerial Cabinet met and found that the Medical, Engineers' and Bar Associations' councils had broken the laws concerning the aims and activities of their professions, and agreed to dissolve the national congresses and assemblies of these associations. In the days that followed, hundreds of lawyers, doctors and engineers were arrested.

According to unconfirmed reports, some of those arrested were executed. Others have since been released, most of them as a result of the December 1991 presidential amnesty. Among those released were Ma'mun Sawwah, a 58-year-old electrical engineer and former company manager, and Ghassan al-Najjar, both former members of the Syrian Engineers' Association who had been in detention since April 1980.

Those who are reported to be still detained include Tawfiq Draq al-Siba'i and Salim Khirbik.

Tawfiq Draq al-Siba'i, a doctor, was detained in Homs in May 1980 after the Syrian censors intercepted a letter from his relatives in Saudi Arabia. The letter expressed concern about the political situation in Syria. On 2 June he was taken from prison in Homs to an unknown destination. When questioned by relatives, the Homs prison authorities denied knowledge of his whereabouts. In November 1986 Amnesty International learned that he was detained in al-Mezze Military Prison, reportedly for involvement in matters affecting state security. Aged about 46, he is married and has five children. He studied medicine at Damascus University and in 1973 went to Montreal, Canada to undertake graduate studies in neurology. He opened a medical clinic in Homs on his return to Syria.

Salim Khirbik, an engineer aged about 43, is reported to be held in 'Adra Prison. A former employee of the national Syrian airline and member of the Syrian Engineers' Association, he has been in detention since his arrest in June 1980.

3

Prisoners held beyond expiry of sentence

At least six people are reported to be still detained despite having served their prison sentences. Four of them are former military staff and two are believed to have been arrested in connection with the Muslim Brotherhood.

Three of the four former military staff — Mahmud Muhammad al-Fayyad, Mustafa Tawfiq Fallah and Jalal al-Din Mustafa Mirhij — were arrested in May 1970. They were among a group of about 350 civilian and military detainees brought before the Supreme State Security Court in a mass trial in August 1971. They were charged with "offences against the security of the state and public order". They were accused of plotting to overthrow the 1966-to-1970 government in Syria and of attempting to reinstate those removed from power in 1966. The official indictment accused them of receiving help from Iraq. Jalal al-Din Mustafa Mirhij and Mustafa Tawfiq Fallah were sentenced to 15 years' imprisonment. Mahmud Muhammad al-Fayyad was sentenced to life imprisonment, commuted to 15 years in November 1971.

On expiry of their sentences in May 1985, the three were transferred to a detention centre in Damascus. They were returned to al-Mezze Military Prison in October 1985 where they remain held without further charges being brought against them. All three are reported to be ill; Mahmud Muhammad al-Fayyad is said to suffer from a gastric ulcer and inflammation of the oesophagus, and to have been denied proper medical attention.

The fourth detainee, Khalil Brayez, a 59-year-old former captain and intelligence officer in the Syrian army, was abducted from Lebanon by Syrian security forces in October or early November 1970. He was dismissed from the army following two short periods of detention in 1962 and 1963 and had been living in Lebanon since 1964 to avoid further arrest. Shortly after the June 1967 war with Israel, he wrote two books, *The Fall of the Golan* and *From the Golan Files*, which were published in Lebanon. Both books were highly critical of the Syrian army's performance during the 1967 war. He was preparing a third book on the same subject at the time of his abduction.

He was initially held in al-Mezze Military Prison and is said to have been tortured during the early period of his detention. His family, however, did not know where he was until 1973, when they were allowed to visit him once a month. It was then learned that he had been sentenced to 15 years' imprisonment in March 1972 following his conviction for incitement to commit murder, incitement to carry out terrorist activities in Syria, and misusing information available to him as an officer in the armed forces. No information about his trial is available. However, despite the expiry of his sentence in October 1985 he remains in detention. Since his arrest he has been held in different prisons, but he is currently believed to be in al-Mezze Prison.

Two people believed to have been imprisoned on suspicion of being members or sympathizers of the Muslim Brotherhood are also still apparently held after expiry of their sentences. Mahmud Oliwi, who is aged about 42 and is married with two children, was arrested on 15 June 1984 in Hama by members of *al-Mukhabarat al-'Askariyya*. He was reportedly suspected of having been involved in the Hama unrest of 1982. In 1985 he was apparently tried and sentenced to one year's imprisonment. No details are available regarding the exact charges brought against him or the trial proceedings. However, he has recently been reported to be still held despite the expiry of his sentence. He is believed to be detained by *al-Mukhabarat al-'Askariyya* in Damascus and no further charges are known to have been brought against him.

Muhammad Jamal Tayyem, a 33-year-old Jordanian and former student of engineering at the University of Aleppo, was arrested in February 1980 reportedly on suspicion of being a member of the Muslim Brotherhood. He was apparently tried before a military court in Damascus and sentenced to 10 years' imprisonment. Amnesty International does not have any details about the charges brought against him or about the trial proceedings. However, he is said to have had no access to a lawyer and since his arrest has been

CHAPTER 3

Mahmud Muhammad al-Fayyad was arrested in 1970 and convicted the following year to 15 years' imprisonment. He remains in prison despite the expiry of his sentence in May 1985 without further charges being brought against him.

Khalil Brayez, now aged about 60, is still imprisoned despite having served his 15-year prison sentence. He was due for release in 1985 and has not been charged with further offences.

SYRIA

visited only once, in 1980, by his mother. In 1985 the Syrian Foreign Ministry apparently informed his family in Jordan that he was alive, but did not give details about his whereabouts or the reasons and conditions of his detention. His sentence expired in 1990, but he has not been released and no further charges are known to have been brought against him.

4

Torture and deaths in custody since 1987

The systematic use of arbitrary arrest and incommunicado detention have provided the context for torture to be a routine and widespread practice in Syrian prisons and detention centres. Although Syria is not a State Party to the UN Convention against Torture and Other Cruel, Inhuman or Degrading Treatment or Punishment [4], torture is banned by the Constitution [5] and under the Penal Code is punishable by imprisonment [6]. However, Amnesty International is not aware of any cases where these laws have actually been implemented, despite repeated and consistent allegations of torture.

In many of the cases of prisoners who have died in custody over the years, torture has been alleged as the main or contributing cause. A pattern of torture in Syria has regularly been highlighted by Amnesty International in its various publications, notably in its two major reports: *Report from Amnesty International to the Government of the Syrian Arab Republic* (AI Index: MDE 24/04/83, November 1983) and *Syria: Torture by the Security Forces* (AI Index: MDE 24/09/87, October 1987). These publications contain first-hand testimonies from torture victims and detailed accounts of the various types of torture used.

According to recent testimonies given to Amnesty International by former political detainees who were released in 1991, torture continues to be routine and widespread. It is used by various security agencies both as a means of extracting information about political suspects and as a form of punishment. Former detainees interviewed recently by Amnesty International showed scars on their bodies and described various methods of torture which they said had caused the scars, including beatings on all parts of the body; *falaqa* (beating on the soles of the feet); *dullab*

SYRIA

(the tyre method — hanging the victim from a suspended tyre and beating him or her with sticks and cables); and pouring cold water over the victim's body.

Among those alleged to have died as a result of torture in recent years are:

- Munir al-Ahmad, a 60-year-old poet and journalist, married with four children, who died on 23 January 1992 while in detention. His body was returned to his family on 2 February. He was reportedly arrested by members of *al-Mukhabarat al-'Askariyya* on 17 June 1991 at his home in Damascus, two days after his return from a visit to Switzerland. He was apparently suspected of having criticized the Syrian Government while on this visit. In March 1992 Amnesty International sought clarification from the Syrian Ministry of Justice regarding allegations of torture and the circumstances surrounding Munir al-Ahmad's death, but had not received a response by late May.

- Colonel Muhammad Dawud (also known as Abu Dawud), a 48-year-old senior member of the Palestine Liberation Organization (PLO), died in his cell in Saidnaya Prison in December 1990 or January 1991, according to former detainees. He had allegedly been subjected to severe torture the previous day. The reasons for his torture were reportedly related to a chant sung by Palestinian and other prisoners in celebration of the anniversary of the Palestinian Revolution, which began in January 1965, and the *intifada* (uprising) in the Occupied Territories, which began in December 1987. He was apparently suspected of being the instigator of the singing. He had reportedly been in detention since 1985.

- Ziad Musa Qatnani reportedly died on 8 May 1990 in *Fara' al-Tahqiq al-'Askari* in Damascus. He was arrested at Damascus airport in July 1985 on arrival from Tunis. He was visited by his mother one month before his death, when he appeared to be in reasonable health. However, when his body was returned to his family, it apparently bore marks of torture by electricity and his skull was broken.

- Munir Francis, a civil engineer aged about 30, reportedly died as a result of torture in April 1990 after he was admitted to al-Muwassat Civil Hospital in Damascus suffering from internal bleeding. According to reports received by Amnesty International, when his coffin was returned to his family his body bore

CHAPTER 4

'Abd al-Razzaq Abazid, a 41-year-old political prisoner, died in custody in April 1988, reportedly as a result of torture. No investigation into the circumstances of his death is known to have been carried out by the authorities.

the marks of beatings. Munir Francis was reportedly arrested, along with others, in Yabrud (al-Nabak), north of Damascus, at the end of March 1990, after anti-government slogans were written on the walls of the town. Apparently one such slogan read: "Yesterday Ceausescu Romania, tomorrow Ceausescu Syria". The arrests were reportedly carried out by members of *al-Amn al-Siyassi*.

- 'Abd al-Razzaq Abazid, a 41-year-old political prisoner, died between 20 and 22 April 1988, reportedly as a result of torture. He is believed to have died in *Fara' al-Tahqiq al-'Askari* and his body was returned to his family on 23 April 1988. He was arrested in February that year by members of *al-Amn al-Siyassi* as a suspected member of the CPPB. He was initially held in Dar'a town for one month, then transferred to *Fara' al-Tahqiq al-'Askari* in Damascus.

- Muhammad al-'Arraj, a teacher born in Lataqiyya, died in *Fara' Falastin* in late December 1987 or early January 1988. A member of the PCA, he was arrested in October 1987 and held in *Fara' Falastin*.

5

Conclusions and Amnesty International's proposals

Amnesty International welcomes the recent presidential amnesties and the release of around 2,000 political prisoners, including prisoners of conscience. But it remains concerned that thousands of others are still held and that the basic pattern of human rights violations in Syria remains unchanged. The state of emergency provides a legal context for the detention without trial or after unfair trials of thousands of political prisoners, including prisoners of conscience, and for widespread and systematic abuse of human rights.

President Assad himself acknowledged in a speech to the People's Assembly on 8 March 1978 that the state of emergency had been used abusively to arrest and detain government opponents. This speech was followed by the release of a number of untried detainees, but they did not include political detainees, mostly people held for minor offences.

In January 1980 the Regional Command of the Ba'th Party established a committee to review the position of all untried detainees held under state of emergency legislation. Shortly afterwards over 150 political detainees were released, but hundreds remained in jail and thousands of other political suspects were arrested in the following months and kept in detention. Amnesty International welcomed the announcement of the review and requested information about specific detainees whose cases should have been included, but received no response. Subsequent repeated requests for information about political detainees and any reviews of their cases have been made to the Syrian authorities by Amnesty International, but without any substantive response.

Most political prisoners are detained without charge or trial: many are or appear to be

CHAPTER 5

prisoners of conscience who are being held solely for the non-violent expression of their conscientiously-held beliefs. All are denied the most basic prisoners' rights guaranteed by international standards, in breach of solemn obligations undertaken by Syria as a State Party to the International Covenant on Civil and Political Rights (ICCPR) — such as the right to contact a lawyer and the right to be brought before a judge and have the opportunity to challenge the legal basis for detention. The majority have been held in these conditions for years — some for over two decades.

Such lengthy detention without trial, in Amnesty International's opinion, is an arbitrary punishment which constitutes a gross violation of international human rights standards, particularly Articles 9(1) and 14(2) and (3)(a) (c) of the ICCPR, to which Syria is a State Party[7]. Article 9(1) provides that:

"Everyone has the right to liberty and security of person. No one shall be subjected to arbitrary arrest or detention. No one shall be deprived of his liberty except on such grounds and in accordance with such procedure as are established by law."

Article 14(2) and (3)(a) (c) state that:

"2. Everyone charged with a criminal offence shall have the right to be presumed innocent until proved guilty according to law.

3. In the determination of any criminal charge against him, everyone shall be entitled to the following minimum guarantees, in full equality:

(a) To be informed promptly and in detail in a language which he understands of the nature and cause of the charge against him;

(c) To be tried without undue delay;"

None of the detainees is said to have been allowed access to a lawyer, as guaranteed by international standards such as Article 14(3)(b) of the ICCPR; Principles 15, 17(1) and 18(1 to 4) of the UN Body of Principles for the Protection of All Persons under Any Form of Detention or Imprisonment (UN Body of Principles); and Rule 93 of the UN Standard Minimum Rules for the Treatment of Prisoners[8]. For example, Principle 17(1) of the UN Body of Principles states that:

35

SYRIA

> "A detained person shall be entitled to have the assistance of a legal counsel. He shall be informed of his right by the competent authority promptly after arrest and shall be provided with reasonable facilities for exercising it."

Under the Syrian Code of Criminal Procedures, legal access is guaranteed by Article 72(2). The Article provides that a detainee is entitled to contact his or her lawyer at any time and in private, except in cases of espionage. In these, defendants are denied legal assistance when they appear before the investigating judge[9].

Similarly, none of the untried political detainees whose cases are known to Amnesty International is ever known to have appeared before a judge, to have been provided with a judicial review of her or his detention, or to have been offered the opportunity to challenge the lawfulness of her or his detention. This violates international human rights standards as well as Syria's own laws. Under international human rights standards, the right to be brought promptly before a judge is guaranteed by Article 9(3) of the ICCPR which states:

> "Anyone arrested or detained on a criminal charge shall be brought promptly before a judge or other officer authorized by law to exercise judicial power..."

Principles 11(1) and 37 of the UN Body of Principles contain similar guarantees[10].

According to the Human Rights Committee's General Comment 8 of the ICCPR, delay in bringing a detainee before a judge should not exceed "a few days". Article 104(1) and (2) of the Syrian Code of Criminal Procedures provides that a detained person must be interrogated by a judge within 24 hours, and that failure to do so renders him or her legally entitled to immediate release. According to Article 105 of the same code, if the detainee is kept in custody for more than 24 hours without having appeared before a judge, the authority holding him or her will be doing so arbitrarily and will be liable for prosecution for the crime of deprivation of personal liberty, as stipulated by Article 358 of the Penal Code. This crime is punishable by imprisonment of one to three years. However, despite the widespread and consistent breaching of this Article by the arresting authorities, Amnesty International is not aware of a single offender ever having been prosecuted.

The detainees' right to a judicial review and to challenge the lawfulness of their detention is contained in Article 9(4) of the ICCPR and Principles 32(1) and 37 of the UN Body of Principles[11]. The UN Special Rapporteur on torture has recognized in his most recent annual report that under Principle 32 this right applies at all times, even in states of emergency:

> *"Each detained person should have the right to initiate, immediately after his arrest, proceedings before a court on the lawfulness of his detention, in conformity with Article 9, paragraph 4 of the ICCPR. Since the Body of Principles, which in Principle 32 contains the same provision, makes no exception for times of emergency, a detained person should be entitled to exercise this right also under a state of siege or emergency."*

Of the few prisoners who have been tried, some are being held beyond the expiry of their sentences without any further charges being brought against them. Others are serving sentences imposed after trials which fell short of international standards. Most of these trials have been held in secrecy before special courts and very little information is available about them. Defendants have frequently been denied assistance by a defence lawyer and not allowed to appeal against conviction and sentence. Such practice is contrary to Article 14 of the ICCPR, particularly paragraphs (1), (3)(b and d) and (5). Paragraph (1) guarantees for everyone the right to a fair and public hearing by a competent, independent and impartial tribunal established by law. Paragraphs (3)(b) and (d) guarantee the right to adequate defence by requiring the effective implementation of the following minimum safeguards for everyone:

> *"3(b) To have adequate time and facilities for the preparation of his defence and to communicate with counsel of his own choosing;*
>
> *(d) To be tried in his presence, and to defend himself in person or through legal assistance of his own choosing; to be informed, if he does not have legal assistance, of this right; and to have legal assistance assigned to him, in any case where the interests of justice so require, and without payment by him in any such case if he does not have sufficient means to pay for it;"*

Paragraph (5) guarantees the right of appeal:

> *"Everyone convicted of a crime shall have the right to*

> *his conviction and sentence being reviewed by a higher tribunal according to law."*

The prisoners whose cases are known to Amnesty International are all believed to have been detained incommunicado for lengthy periods following their arrest. Some have apparently been held in this condition throughout years of detention. The whereabouts of many of them today, often years after they were arrested, are still unknown even to their closest relatives. Yet access to the outside world is guaranteed by international standards as a fundamental individual human right and a safeguard against torture. The prisoner's right to communicate without delay with his or her family is guaranteed by Principle 16(1) of the UN Body of Principles and Rule 92 of the UN Standard Minimum Rules. Principle 16(1) states:

> *"Promptly after arrest and after each transfer from one place of detention or imprisonment to another, a detained or imprisoned person shall be entitled to notify or require the competent authority to notify members of his family or other appropriate persons of his choice of his arrest, detention or imprisonment or of the transfer and of the place where he is kept in custody."*

Rule 92 states that: "An untried prisoner shall be allowed to inform immediately his family of his detention and shall be given all reasonable facilities for communicating with his family and friends, and for receiving visits from them, subject only to restrictions and supervision as are necessary in the interests of the administration of justice and of the security and good order of the institution."

Principle 15 of the UN Body of Principles makes clear that the right to communicate with one's family may not be denied for more than a matter of days, even in exceptional cases.

Detainees have also routinely been denied prompt and regular access to doctors, although this is guaranteed as a right by a number of international human rights standards, including Rule 24 of the UN Standard Minimum Rules, Principle 24 of the Body of Principles, and Article 6 of the UN Code of Conduct for Law Enforcement Officials. For example, Principle 24 of the UN Body of Principles requires that:

> *"A proper medical examination shall be offered to a detained or imprisoned person as promptly as possible*

CHAPTER 5

after his admission to the place of detention or imprisonment, and thereafter medical care and treatment shall be provided whenever necessary."[12]

The violation of these rights has had dramatic consequences for the moral and physical integrity of prisoners. Most are reported to have been tortured or ill-treated while being held in incommunicado detention. Many have, as a result, sustained serious long-term injuries. Yet all the evidence continues to suggest that they are denied access to adequate medical treatment and facilities.

Torture is a crime under Article 28(3) of the Syrian Constitution of 1973, and is punishable by imprisonment under Article 391 of the Penal Code. Yet in practice, none of those responsible for torture is known to have been brought to trial. Moreover, no victim of torture is known to have been offered rehabilitation facilities or compensation.

Amnesty International has repeatedly over many years made known to the Syrian authorities its concern about the gross and widespread human rights violations which have been committed in the country. It has continued to press for the immediate and unconditional release of all prisoners of conscience, and the fair and prompt trial or release of other political prisoners. It has repeatedly urged the Syrian Government to live up to its obligation to stop torture, calling for all torture allegations to be thoroughly and impartially investigated, and for the perpetrators of torture to be identified and brought to justice. The organization has also repeatedly sought assurances that all prisoners are treated humanely, given regular access to family members and lawyers, and given adequate medical care. No substantive response has been received from the Syrian authorities.

Amnesty International's proposals

Amnesty International believes that, despite the welcome presidential amnesties and the mass release of prisoners of conscience and political prisoners, much more needs to be done to stop the continuing and widespread abuse of the rights of untried detainees and sentenced prisoners in Syria.

It calls on the Syrian authorities to take the following urgent steps:

- immediately and unconditionally release all prisoners of conscience;
- release all political prisoners held without trial and all those detained beyond the expiry of their sentence unless they are charged with a recognizably criminal offence and given a prompt and fair trial as required by Article 14 of the ICCPR;
- immediately introduce a procedure whereby the families of all detainees are automatically informed of the whereabouts of their detained relatives and allowed prompt access to them;
- stop torture — by ensuring that the preventive and prohibitive penal laws intended as safeguards against such an inhumane practice are rigorously implemented and their application monitored.

Amnesty International also calls for the urgent implementation of at least the following investigative actions. The authorities should:

- set up an independent and impartial body to investigate all allegations of torture and deaths in custody, and make the findings public: such investigations should be consistent with standards such as the UN Principles on the Effective Prevention and Investigation of Extra-Legal, Arbitrary and Summary Executions;
- ensure that those responsible for torture are brought to justice in accordance with the requirements of international standards;
- ensure that each torture victim obtains redress and has an enforceable right to fair and adequate compensation, including the means for as full a rehabilitation as possible.

In addition, Amnesty International urges the authorities to introduce safeguards to protect human rights. It should:

- ensure that arrests are carried out with a judicial warrant and are always supervised by the judiciary;
- ensure that detained or imprisoned people are given prompt and regular access to family, lawyers and doctors, with whom they should be able to communicate in private;
- ensure that all political detainees have prompt access to a judge as required both by international standards and Articles 104 and 105 of the Syrian Code of Criminal Procedures;

CHAPTER 5

- ensure that arresting authorities and the various security forces are issued with instructions that torture and ill-treatment of any person in their custody is strictly prohibited, and any alleged breach of such instructions will be investigated and those found guilty will be punished;
- ratify the UN Convention against Torture and Other Cruel, Inhuman or Degrading Treatment or Punishment and the First Optional Protocol to the International Covenant on Civil and Political Rights (ICCPR);
- enact a law implementing Article 9(4) of the ICCPR which provides the right to challenge the legality of detention and to obtain release when the detention is unlawful;
- enact a law guaranteeing the right to appeal in all cases.

SYRIA

ENDNOTES

Introduction

[1] The Human Rights Committee, the body of experts which monitors implementation of the International Covenant on Civil and Political Rights, to which Syria acceded in April 1969, observed in its General Comment 5 (13) that "measures taken under Article 4 [permitting emergency legislation] are of an exceptional and temporary nature and may only last as long as the life of the nation concerned is threatened and that in times of emergency, the protection of human rights becomes all the more important, particularly those rights from which no derogation can be made".

Chapter 1

[2] The Supreme State Security Court was introduced by Legislative Decree No.47 of 28 March 1968 entitled: Creation of "a Supreme State Security" Court and delineation of its jurisdiction. It replaced the exceptional Military Courts introduced by Legislative Decree No.6 of 7 January 1965 and amended by Legislative Decree No.108 of 10 June 1965, retaining their jurisdiction. It specialises in the trial of offences contained in Article 3 of Legislative Decree No.6 of 7 January 1965 which include: acts contrary to the socialist system of the state [Paras(a)(b)]; state security offences contained in Articles 291 to 311 of the Penal Code [Para(c)]; contravention of martial law governor's orders [Para(d)]; activity contrary to the unity of Arab countries or to the goals of the revolution, carried out by means of demonstration, assembly, incitement, or dissemination of false information intended to cause anxiety and shake the confidence of the masses in the aims of the revolution [Para(e)]; receiving money or any donations in order to carry out activities against the aims of the revolution of 8 March 1963 [Para(f)]; attacks on religious places or state institutions, and incitement to religious or racial sectarianism as well as to demonstrations and looting [Para(g)]. The punishment for these offences, which is contained in Article 4 of the same Legislative Decree, ranges from imprisonment with hard labour to the death penalty.

[3] Article 8 of Legislative Decree No. 47 of 28 March 1968 states explicitly that appeal is not allowed against Supreme State Security Court decisions. However, it provides that all such decisions do not come into force before they are ratified by the President.

Chapter 4

[4] In March 1986, a Syrian representative announced before the 42nd session of the United Nations Commission on Human Rights his government's intention to accede to the Convention against Torture, but so far it has not done so.

[5] Article 28(3) of the 1973 Constitution states that: "No one shall be subjected to physical or moral torture or to humiliating treatment. The law shall define the penalties for such actions."

[6] In accordance with Article 391 of the Syrian Penal Code, any person who subjects another to any form of violence not permissible under the law for the purpose of obtaining a confession or information relating to an offence is liable to imprisonment for between three months and three years. If the violent act results in illness or injury to the victim, the law prescribes a minimum of one year's imprisonment for the offender.

ENDNOTES

Chapter 5
[7] **International Covenant on Civil and Political Rights**

Article 9

1. Everyone has the right to liberty and security of person. No one shall be subjected to arbitrary arrest or detention. No one shall be deprived of his liberty except on such grounds and in accordance with such procedure as are established by law.

2. Anyone who is arrested shall be informed, at the time of arrest, of the reasons for his arrest and shall be promptly informed of any charges against him.

3. Anyone arrested or detained on a criminal charge shall be brought promptly before a judge or other officer authorized by law to exercise judicial power and shall be entitled to trial within a reasonable time or to release. It shall not be the general rule that persons awaiting trial shall be detained in custody, but release may be subject to guarantees to appear for trial, at any other stage of the judicial proceedings, and, should occasion arise, for execution of the judgement.

4. Anyone who is deprived of his liberty by arrest or detention shall be entitled to take proceedings before a court, in order that that court may decide without delay on the lawfulness of his detention and order his release if the detention is not lawful.

5. Anyone who has been victim of unlawful arrest or detention shall have an enforceable right to compensation.

Article 14

1. All persons shall be equal before the courts and tribunals. In the determination of any criminal charge against him, or of his rights and obligations in a suit at law, everyone shall be entitled to a fair and public hearing by a competent, independent and impartial tribunal established by law. The press and the public may be excluded from all or part of a trial for reasons of morals, public order (*ordre public*) or national security in a democratic society, or when the interest of the private lives of the Parties so requires, or to the extent strictly necessary in the opinion of the court in special circumstances where publicity would prejudice the interests of justice; but any judgement rendered in a criminal case or in a suit at law shall be made public except where the interest of juvenile persons otherwise requires or the proceedings concern matrimonial disputes of the guardianship of children.

2. Everyone charged with a criminal offence shall have the right to be presumed innocent until proved guilty according to law.

3. In the determination of any criminal charge against him, everyone shall be entitled to the following minimum guarantees, in full equality:

(a) To be informed promptly and in detail in a language which he understands of the nature and cause of the charge against him;

(b) To have adequate time and facilities for the preparation of his defence and to communicate with counsel of his own choosing;

(c) To be tried without undue delay;

(d) To be tried in his presence, and to defend himself in person or through

SYRIA

legal assistance of his own choosing; to be informed, if he does not have legal assistance, of this right; and to have legal assistance assigned to him, in any case where the interests of justice so require, and without payment by him in any such case if he does not have sufficient means to pay for it;

(e) To examine, or have examined, the witnesses against him and to obtain the attendance and examination of witnesses on his behalf under the same conditions as witnesses against him;

(f) To have the free assistance of an interpreter if he cannot understand or speak the language used in court;

(g) Not to be compelled to testify against himself or to confess guilt.

4. In the case of juvenile persons, the procedure shall be such as will take account of their age and the desirability of promoting their rehabilitation.

5. Everyone convicted of a crime shall have the right to his conviction and sentence being reviewed by a higher tribunal according to law.

6. When a person has by a final decision been convicted of a criminal offence and when subsequently his conviction has been reversed or he has been pardoned on the ground that a new or newly discovered fact shows conclusively that there has been a miscarriage of justice, the person who has suffered punishment as a result of such conviction shall be compensated according to law, unless it is proved that the non-disclosure of the unknown fact in time is wholly or partly attributable to him.

7. No one shall be liable to be tried or punished again for an offence for which he has already been finally convicted or acquitted in accordance with the law and penal procedure of each country.

[8] **UN Standard Minimum Rules for the Treatment of Prisoners**
Rule 93. For the purposes of his defence, an untried prisoner shall be allowed to apply for free legal aid where such aid is available, and to receive visits from his legal adviser with a view to his defence and to prepare and hand to him confidential instructions. For these purposes, he shall if he so desires be supplied with writing material. Interviews between the prisoner and his legal adviser may be within sight but not within the hearing of a police or institution official.

UN Body of Principles for the Protection of All Persons under Any Form of Detention or Imprisonment

Principle 15
    Notwithstanding the exceptions contained in principle 16, paragraph 4 and principle 18, paragraph 3, communication of the detained or imprisoned person with the outside world, and in particular his family or counsel, shall not be denied for more than a matter of days.

Principle 18
    1. A detained or imprisoned person shall be entitled to communicate and consult with his legal counsel.

    2. A detained or imprisoned person shall be allowed adequate time and facilities for consultations with his legal counsel.

    3. The right of a detained or imprisoned person to be visited by and to consult and communicate, without delay or censorship and in full confidentiality, with his legal counsel may not be suspended or restricted save in exceptional

ENDNOTES

circumstances, to be specified by law or lawful regulations, when it is considered indispensable by a judicial or other authority in order to maintain security and good order.

4. Interviews between a detained or imprisoned person and his legal counsel may be within sight, but not within the hearing, of a law enforcement official.

5. Communications between a detained or imprisoned person and his legal counsel mentioned in the present principle shall be inadmissible as evidence against the detained or imprisoned person unless they are connected with a continuing or contemplated crime.

[9] This exception is contained in Article 1 of Legislative Decree No. 5 of 26 February 1952.

[10] Principle 11(1) states: "A person shall not be kept in detention without being given an effective opportunity to be heard promptly by a judicial or other authority. A detained person shall have the right to defend himself or to be assisted by counsel as prescribed by law."

Principle 37 states: "A person detained on a criminal charge shall be brought before a judicial or other authority provided by law promptly after his arrest. Such authority shall decide without delay upon the lawfulness and necessity of detention. No person may be kept under detention pending investigation or trial except upon the written order of such an authority. A detained person shall, when brought before such an authority, have the right to make a statement on the treatment received by him while in custody.

[11] **UN Body of Principles for the Protection of All Persons under Any Form of Detention or Imprisonment**

Principle 32
   1. A detained person or his counsel shall be entitled at any time to take proceedings according to domestic law before a judicial or other authority to challenge the lawfulness of his detention in order to obtain his release without delay; if it is unlawful.

   2. The proceedings referred to in paragraph 1 of the present principle shall be simple and expeditious and at no cost for the detained persons without adequate means. The detaining authority shall produce without unreasonable delay the detained person before the reviewing authority.

[12] Article 6 of the UN Code of Conduct for Law Enforcement Officials, adopted by the UN General Assembly resolution 34/169 of 17 December 1979, provides that: "Law enforcement officials shall ensure the full protection of the health of persons in their custody and, in particular, shall take immediate action to secure medical attention whenever required."

Rule 24 of the Standard Minimum Rules for the Treatment of Prisoners requires that: "The medical officer shall see and examine every prisoner as soon as possible after his admission and thereafter as necessary, with a view particularly to the discovery of physical or mental illness and the taking of all necessary measures; the segregation of prisoners suspected of infectious or contagious conditions; the noting of physical or mental defects which might hamper rehabilitation, and the determination of the physical capacity of every prisoner for work."

SYRIA

APPENDIX

State of emergency laws

Legislative Decree Number 51
(dated 22/12/1962)

Law for a State of Emergency

The Cabinet issued and the President of the Republic broadcast the following legislative decree:

PART ONE

The Proclamation of a State of Emergency

Article 1

a) A state of emergency may be announced in a situation of war or one in which war threatens to break out or one in which public security and order in the territory of the Republic or part of it is exposed to danger through the occurrence of internal disturbances or general catastrophes.

b) The state of emergency can extend to the whole of the Syrian territory or to a part of it.

Article 2

a) The state of emergency shall be proclaimed by a decree from the cabinet, presided over by the President of the Republic. It must be carried by a majority of two thirds and be made known to the Chamber of Deputies at its next meeting.

b) The decree shall define the restrictions and measures which the Martial Law Governor may adopt and which are stipulated in Article 4 of the Legislative Decree without violation of the rulings of Article 5 of the same Decree.

Article 3

a) On proclamation of a state of emergency the President of the Republic shall name a Martial Law Governor and all powers of internal and external security shall be placed at his disposal.

b) The Martial Law Governor shall appoint, by decree, one or two deputies to work with him.

c) The deputies of the Martial Law Governor shall carry out tasks delegated to them in the areas assigned by him.

Article 4

The Martial Law governor or his deputy shall issue written orders to adopt some or all of the following restrictions and measures and he shall bring anyone who violates them before military court

a) The placing of restrictions on freedom of individuals with respect to meetings, residence, travel and passage in specific places or at particular times. Preventive arrest of anyone suspected of endangering public security and order. Authorization to investigate persons and places. Delegation of any person to perform any of these tasks.

b) The censorship of letters and communications of all kinds. Censorship of newspapers, periodicals, publications, drawings, printed matter, broadcasts

APPENDIX

and all means of communication, propaganda and publicity before issue; also their seizure, confiscation and suspension, the denial of their rights and the closure of the places in which they were printed.

c) The fixing of opening and closing times for public places.

d) The withdrawal of licenses for weapons, ammunition and all kinds of explosives and the ordering of their surrender and seizure. The closure of weapons stores.

e) The evacuation of areas or their isolation, the organization of the means of transport, the restriction of communications and their limitation between areas.

f) The requisitioning of movable property and real estate and the temporary sequestration of companies and establishments with delay in the settlement of debts and obligations due either to or from the requisitioned body.

g) The imposition of punishments for the contravention of these orders provided these do not exceed three years' imprisonment and 3,000 lira or either of these two. If an order does not impose the punishment for the contravention of its rulings, such contravention shall be punished with imprisonment for not more than six months and a fine of not more than 500 lira or with one of the two. This all being with the proviso that the maximum penalties specified in other laws are not exceeded.

Article 5

a) Where necessary the cabinet, in session under the chairmanship of the President of the Republic, may extend the field of the restrictions and measures listed in the previous paragraph through a decree to be submitted to the Chamber of Deputies at its first meeting.

b) The cabinet may also limit the field of the restrictions and measures referred to in accordance with the situation which called for the announcement of the state of emergency.

Article 6

In the areas where a state of emergency has been declared the following offences shall be referred to military courts whatever the rank of those who committed them, incited their commission or participated in them.

a) Contravention of orders issued by the Martial Law Governor.

b) Offences against the security of the state and public order (Articles 260 - 339 of the Penal Code).*

c) Offences against public authority (Articles 369 - 387).**

d) Offences which disturb public confidence (Articles 427 - 459).**

e) Offences which constitute a general danger (Article 573 - 586).

Article 7

The Martial Law Governor may exempt some of the offences defined in the previous article from the jurisdiction of military courts.

Article 8

Where there is a dispute regarding jurisdiction between civil and military courts the Martial Law Governor shall act as final arbiter.

SYRIA

Article 9
Death sentences in the process of confirmation shall only be carried out where they have been approved by the Martial Law Governor after he has consulted the pardons committee of the Ministry of Justice.

PART TWO
The Termination of a State of Emergency

Article 10
The state of emergency shall be terminated by the authority responsible for proclaiming it in accordance with the provisions in Article 2 of this legislative decree.

Article 11
After the termination of the state of emergency military courts shall continue to deal with cases within their jurisdiction whether or not they are assigned to them.

PART THREE
Temporary Rulings

Article 12
State of Emergency Law number 162 of 27/9/1958 with all its amendments is hereby cancelled.

Article 13
a) In all cases the state of emergency courts created by Law 162 shall remain competent to try offences within their jurisdiction which were committed before the issuing of this legislative decree whether or not they are assigned to them.

In the matters of investigation, assignment, trial, suspension of trial, confirmation or alteration of rulings issued or due to be issued they shall follow the principles and procedures that are followed in accordance with that law.

The President of the Republic or whomsoever he delegates may suspend a judicial investigation while it is at the courts.*

b) The sequestration imposed on certain firms and establishments in accordance with Law 162 shall remain in force until it is cancelled by a decree passed by the cabinet.

c) The state of emergency announced on the basis of Law 162 shall be considered to remain in force until its abolition is completed in accordance with Article 10 of this legislative decree.

Article 14
This legislative decree shall be published and shall take effect from the day of its being issued.

Damascus 26/8/1382 (=22/12/1962)

* Amended by Legislative Decree No. 1 of 9/3/1963.

* Amr 'Urfi (Martial Law Order) No. 16 of 17 June 1966 amended this and refers offences under Articles 314 and 318 to the relevant civil courts.

** Amr 'Urfi No. 31 of August 1965 has amended this Article and refers these offences to the relevant civil courts.